YELLOW ARROW

Vol. V, No. 3
Fall 2020
(Re)Formation

Yellow Arrow Journal

Creative nonfiction, poetry, book reviews, and cover art
by writers/artists that identify as women

Vol. V, No. 3
Fall 2020
(Re)Formation

Editor-in-Chief
Kapua Iao

Poetry Editor
Ann Quinn

Editorial Associates
Bailey Drumm, Brenna Ebner, Kierstin Kessler,
Alexa Laharty, and Siobhan McKenna

Contributors
Colleen Anderson, Amy L. Bernstein, Chris Biles, Ute Carson,
Chiazo V., Meg Crane, RC deWinter, Bailey Drumm,
LynneAnne Forest, Priscilla Frake, Paulina Freedman,
Charity R. Bartley Howard, Sarah Iler, Siobhan McKenna,
Katie Mitchell, Katie Murray, Anna Nissley, Nikita Rimal Sharma,
Deja Ryland, Kathryn Sadakierski, Saige Thornley,
Keshni Naicker Washington, Aressa V. Williams,
and Glenna D. Wolfe

Cover Art
Jeanne Quinn

YELLOW ARROW
PUBLISHING
PO Box 12119, Baltimore, MD 21281
info@yellowarrowpublishing.com

Yellow Arrow Journal - (Re)Formation
Copyright © 2020 by Yellow Arrow Publishing
All rights reserved.

ISBN (paperback): 978-1-7350230-3-8
ISSN (print): 2688-3015
ISSN (online): 2688-3023

Cover art by Jeanne Quinn.
Cover and interior design by Yellow Arrow Publishing.
For more information, see yellowarrowpublishing.com.

*We prioritize the unique voice and
style of each of our authors.*

*Every writer has a story to tell and
every story is worth telling.*

Yellow Arrow Publishing

Panes
Priscilla Frake

The poem arrives with its own blueprint,
its own lumber and hardware.
It has to. It's only a window

built out of words, only part of a wall.
It has to construct itself out of solid brick
and vague dissatisfaction.

The poem is not a bay window
or a set of French doors,
but a narrow view sliced from a dormer.

The distant hills wobble
as I look through its wavering pane
to where lights are troweled along the horizon

scraped over textured grass. The poem
opens to this light and stays open
long after darkness has fallen.

formation : construction

Table of Contents

Dear Readers,

"I think of the trees and how simply they let go . . ." From The Journals of May Sarton Volume One: Journal of a Solitude, Plant Dreaming Deep, and Recovering by May Sarton

One of my favorite times of the year is the month of September. Living in Baltimore, it is then that I begin to feel the heat and humidity of the summer give way to the cooler breezes of the coming season. This year—this epic year—I noticed with special attention the leaves starting to change color and fall, letting go after all of their hard work. On September 22, as a part of the natural cycle and rhythm of life, we officially moved into autumn.

Each season, Gaia, Mother Earth, offers us magnificent gifts. In the autumn, she, with beauty and inspiration, shows us that letting go is a part of life. As each deciduous tree drops its leaves, space is made for the new buds to arrive in the spring. There is a sacredness to the letting go, an understanding of the necessity to do so, a beautiful metaphor.

We have been in a time of great upheaval and change. Already this year, we have had to let go of many things: a usual work routine, freedom to move about as we choose, and a mostly predictable future, to name a few. As painful and grief-filled as this letting go may be, we can trust that this release will allow room for something new to emerge. Perhaps not needing to commute to work has made your mornings more relaxing. Possibly you have found new ways to take care of your health and well-being. Maybe you have even reached out to loved ones in a different and more meaningful way, understanding the fragility of life at an even deeper level. Letting go is a natural process. It is us humans who choose to resist it.

Like many of us individually, Yellow Arrow Publishing is going through our own process of letting go and making space for a new way of being. At the end of August, we shut the doors of Yellow Arrow House. While a sadness fills our hearts for a dream not fully expressed, gratitude abounds for the experiences that Yellow Arrow House brought to us.

With the letting go, comes tremendous opportunity for new growth. We have been inspired to reinvent and (re)form our organization to better serve all women who have the desire to write. What has not changed is our belief that women's voices are powerful and sharing our stories makes a difference, now more than ever.

One final note, you'll notice some additional words at the end of each included piece. Because of the duality of the theme **(Re)Formation**, we were curious which each author focused on and how they interpreted it. May this collection of poems, creative narratives, and book reviews, in this fall edition of the *Yellow Arrow Journal*, inspire us all to surrender what is no longer needed as we speak our truth with glory and create a new world.

Sincerely,

Gina Strauss
Feminine Leadership Advisor, Yellow Arrow Publishing

(RE)FORMATION

Sand
Deja Ryland

"Surrender," they say.
"Accept your impermanence.
 Names hold no weight when you are,
 Designated to return to dust."

*****

Why the waves are pulled back to the sea

My toes gently slip into the warm grains of sand, enfolding perfectly around my foot before engulfing it completely. My dad used to always take my siblings and me to the beach at least once a year.

We have family in Clearwater Beach, Florida, and one summer we stayed with them for a week. My dad, myself, my little brother, Ty, and my older sister, Jenelle, would race each other to see who could get to the water first. We'd jump over the waves, body surf, or sit on the shore and let the waves crash on top of us. Sometimes we'd plant our feet in the sand with our backs to the ocean and feel like we were moving backward as the wave broke, stretching as far as it could toward the shore before rushing back toward the sea.

It wasn't until I'd gotten older that I realized that the water was being pulled back from where it came from. If anything, the sea has taught me that you must always return home.

What the sand has taught me about letting go

Ashes are the only remains left of your previous form. And one day, Dad, we will set you free, spread your ashes across the clearest water we can find, and I will whisper, "You are untethered, Dad." I am still not fully sure how to be at peace with letting you go, but I remind myself that there will always be remnants and pieces of you.

When I was researching sand, I searched through multiple definitions online and one thought seemed to really resonate throughout: sand is a nonrenewable resource over many, many human timescales. Sand is made up of tiny pieces of rock and other materials, weathered down by wind and other forces. However, it is a fact that sand is nonrenewable, that each tiny piece can't be recreated, that each piece remains bound to some previous identity, some previous form. Whether it be quartz or some other rock or mineral. A grain of sand is always tethered to its past life.

The sand comforts me by showing me that there will always be eternal guides that remind us of where we come from—that there is no one form possible to stay in permanently. So that is how I will find comfort in letting you go. The sand reminds me that there are compositions—imperishable histories—that will always align our stories together.

What sand dunes taught me about reunions

According to National Geographic, sand dunes are mounds of sand formed into large pyramidal piles by the wind. Sand dunes remind me that with any travels there will always be a rest stop. That there is purpose in the way each grain is swept into a pile and more than likely, swept away at a later time. Sand dunes are like clusters of I-was-here notes that join together to make one huge statement. So when I ask myself how you will remember me in your next journey, I hope that, like the sand moving from one dune to the next, we, too, will meet somewhere along our travels. So, until we meet again.

Why I will always trust the hourglass instead of the clock

The hourglass, also known as a 'sand clock,' was invented by a French monk named Liutprand in the eighth century. It was built as an instrument to measure the passage of time. Typically, sand is put inside so that its passing from one vial to another demonstrates this change. This was no mistake. At first, people used the hourglass on a daily basis, but it soon became just a prop or house decoration as more and more clocks were created.

April 14, 2019, is the day my father took his last breath. Night after night, I became consumed by anxious thoughts that convinced me I had no time; that I wasn't doing enough with the hours I had. My mind wanted to convince me that time was finite. An alarm clock was set for 8:00 a.m. to wake me up, another for 8:15 in case I missed the first one I'd set, and a third set for 8:30 as a last reminder. But, I still couldn't get out of bed so I'd lie there. I was aware that I had class at 9:30, that I had work immediately following school, yet I was stuck. This was the schedule I repeated Monday through Friday. How ironic it was that I'd put so much effort into sticking to this schedule when all life kept throwing in my face was that no plans could ever really go as planned. That schedules are illusions we use to keep ourselves from going mad. A way to feel like we have control, some kind of order:

> The clock inside the classroom,
> the time on my phone screen,
> the time on the watch face,
> the time on the top right corner of the television screen when I am
>   searching through the guide,
> the time on the bottom right-hand corner of my computer,
>
> and I watch,
> and I check,
> and check again. Everything accessible at a glance.
>   Everything measured in numbers.

Yet the hourglass, lacking any numerical measurement, only measures by the mere passing of grains of sand through a very narrow neck. You flip it over onto the other side and restart the timer. This is why the hourglass is a much more realistic representation of time. The way time slips by as you watch the sand fill the bottom or the sand empty from the top. Similarly to how we watch life, how we watch our pasts and futures fill but are so unaware of that narrow neck, of how many grains of sand have actually passed through, of each individual grain passing through. The tiny narrow neck of the hourglass is actually the most important part to pay attention to.

The hourglass has taught me two things:

> Do not be fooled by man's definition of time.
> Do not bind time to our minuscule human timescales.

This is why I will always trust the hourglass instead of the clock.

✳✳✳✳✳

"Surreal, you are," I respond.
"At last, I understand.
 Naive we are to believe in endings when you
 Dare to show otherwise."

reformation : genesis

Risks Around Each Corner
Ute Carson

"Nothing can be taken for granted when you're 80.
There is risk wherever you turn."
My doctor's warning echoes as I leave the clinic.
Even well-oiled hinges are beginning to creak,
my heart is skipping a beat,
and my feet burn at night.
Getting through an ordinary day saps my energy.
I am drained after even a leisurely walk.
But should I stop dancing because I fear a fall?
Should I leave off lovemaking
lest pleasure stop my heart?
No longer climb a little higher
because I'm short of breath?
Now in old age I pay for excesses of joy
with mounting aches and pains.
But rekindling the thrill of cherished skills
still seems worth it, all in all.
By staying connected through breath and touch
we delay the long sleep that awaits us all.
I have resolved to take risks
while I'm still able to savor life's sweet nectars.

formation : choosing to be formed

Everything Gets Old
Chiazo V.

At 34 years, 6 months, and 29 days, I shouldn't look as old as I do. Though, I don't exactly feel as old as I look. I am fun and playful, young at heart; yet I fear for that heart. Because the weight I drag around is doing more than making me look beyond my age. The weight has brought with it constant bouts of heart palpitations. I had experienced them during each of my three pregnancies spanning across six years. But now they are back, and I'm definitely not expecting. With a little research, I discover that weight has a lot to do with issues of heart palpitations and could be a sign of a potentially serious heart condition. And with the help of the Body Mass Index calculator, I make another astonishing discovery: I am no longer overweight but have crossed into the obese spectrum.

I've been on the plump side for the past couple of years, especially since I started having kids. I've always considered myself curvy, but I never thought I was obese. And I never imagined my weight could pose a serious health threat to me. I only knew I kind of looked older because of it, and that's something I've had to live with for some time. This fact gets more obvious whenever I visit my sister who lives in Enugu, the next city, about 50 minutes by car. We once ran into her colleague when we went shopping at an electrical goods store close to her house, and he called me her aunt. And my sister is four years older than me!

Not too long after this incident, when I next visited her, a longtime acquaintance of the family saw us together and said to her, "This must be your older sister." The man (who happened to be more familiar with my sister) was talking about me . . . again.

I laughed it off, declaring to the mistaken man, "More like the last child."

I have often tried not to let such comments get to me. And they are not to blame, really. After all, my older sister, in all her trim younger-ish glory, is all about eating right, staying fit, and doing all that healthy stuff. And I have yet to lose all the baby fat, a 'mere' three years after having my last child.

Don't get me wrong, I have tried to get my weight under check before. But after losing and then adding a couple extra kilos, I had a conversation with myself and decided that maybe it was time to embrace myself as I am—thick and old-ish. Perhaps, I am one of the few (or many) who can't keep the fat away. Perhaps it is because I am one of the few (or many, again) who can't keep away from the breads. Pastries. Sweets. Cakes. Sodas. And the list goes on. So, for a few blessed, blissful weeks, I embarked on a journey of self-loving body appreciation. I felt free and liberated though the journey was cut rather short.

When, after walking for a few short minutes, I started panting like Usain Bolt after another one of his world record feats, I knew it was time to look my problem in the face and address it. And when the heart palpitations started, the message got even clearer. My problem wasn't just my body size and structure; it was that my body couldn't function like a 34-year-old's should.

And that is what currently bothers me the most. These days, when I look in the mirror, I don't just see a young, curvy woman. I see a woman whose poor lifestyle choices are taking a toll on her body.

And it took a statement from my first son, age 8, to really drive this home. For quite some time now, my boy has been saying, "Everything gets old." He would go on to list the things that get old: toys, cars, and houses . . . and sometimes he would add, "Everyone gets old, too." And I know that I am a big part of that everyone.

Not just that I am getting older as the clock ticks the seconds away, but because I am getting older as I let my body age with my unhealthy choices, faster than the speed of those ticking hands. My body, like any machine, needs to be properly maintained. And this maintenance must go beyond trying out another weight loss recipe. Going on another diet. Regularly exercising. Been there, done that. And will probably have to do it all over again, and again.

But more importantly, I know I need a change that runs deeper than the fat cells padding my organs and blood vessels. I need a thorough transformation.

And the first step is to love myself enough to do the right thing for me and my future. Then, to get back on the horse and whip my body into shape, getting it more functional and fit for my age. And I'm getting there, trying to work up the morale to get me on track to a healthier, happier me.

So, it turns out that I am not doing anything I haven't done before, but rather, am putting things in proper perspective and getting things done in the right order.

Well, baby steps. A little bit every day goes a long way. I haven't given up on me yet. I intend to live this life to the fullest. Live long and live well. And God help me, I intend to get better with age, just like a fine wine. A full-bodied fine wine.

reformation : shape up

Topsoil
Meg Crane

I used to think
I was damned to the seasons—
a frail-boned Persephone:
hands stained with pomegranate pills,
last spring's diagnoses fluttering in my stomach
with every shortened day.

I used to think
I was doomed to hide and hibernate.
Six feet under,
a temporary death;
and each spring I'd claw my way
through the rubble of winter
to heal my bleeding fingernails
in the brighter months.

Now I think
(maybe)
I might be an evergreen.
Now I think
(maybe)
that barren winter earth
could be the perfect place
to plant my roots.
Now I think
(maybe)
these darker nights are just a chance
to see the stars a little longer.

Yes, this light is thin,
but it is still sunshine.
Yes, these times are tough,
but we are still growing.

reformation : renewal

Acorn
Sarah Iler

She told them her dreams
and they offered cheap alternatives
they thought she could afford.

Certain of her smallness
they saw it first hand, painted
as wrinkles of self-doubt across her face.

She received proper baptism
in condescension oozing invisibly
from their eyes. And although

she didn't buy their discounted dreams,
more than ever she, too, was certain
of her smallness. But then she grew

unexpectedly and ever so little
by little. The way an acorn reveals itself
a sprawling oak only after earning time

ring by ring. The result may be
as surprising to the acorn as anyone else.
And although they didn't think much of her

by looking at the seed,
which they mistook for flowering finality,
she grew anyway.

formation : growth

The Ark
LynneAnne Forest

She, too, built an ark,
to survive floods of abuse,
loneliness, despair.
She rode pounding waves,
endured, persisted, until,

as if carrying a green branch of hope,
displaying rainbow's promise,
someone appeared, now visible
through storms of importuning—

Someone who broke through
her longtime fears of drowning.
He appeared—one who could be trusted,
listen, understand, did not abandon,
wise with healing ways.

In time, the storms grew calmer,
the waves smoothed out.
The battered ark approached the shore—
land, rich soil where meaning might grow,
where new consciousness of love could sing.

Standing steady, wooden plank
no longer heaving—
with more hope, quiet knowing,
much gratitude,

she stepped ashore.

formation : becoming

Book Review
Becoming
by Michelle Obama
Reviewed by Bailey Drumm

"Are you enough? Yes." This mantra rings throughout *Becoming* by Michelle Obama,[1] as she navigates the reader through the benefits of being truly, honestly one's intended self. In order to address this, she chose to split her book into three sections: "Becoming Me," which discusses her childhood leading up to her dating Barack Obama; "Becoming Us," which encapsulates the beginning of their relationship up to President Obama's inauguration in 2009; and "Becoming More," which summarizes the Obama family's time spent in the White House. She's been a daughter, a mother, a wife, an attorney, a first lady, and an author, but what Obama assures readers is that being their genuine selves is their most attractive form. That's what others want, and what they should want for themselves. A person will shine once their core being is defined.

Obama opens the book with "Becoming Me," mentioning that she used to love when people would ask her, as a child, what she wanted to be when she grew up, because she had the perfectly constructed answer to impress adults. Now, as an adult, she hates the question, because growing up isn't finite. Who we are, and what we are, are many things. We become different people as the world around us changes, and we form and reform ourselves around it.

After being stuck inside for months, I, as I'm sure many others have, became all too acquainted with my 'alone' self, versus who I became in a crowd. Currently, we are shedding our work masks and learning not to apologize for the inconveniences we have

---

1 Published by Crown Publishing (1st edition, 2018), 448 pages; hardcover (978-1-5247631-3-8) or e-book (978-1-5247631-5-2). For more information, visit Becomingmichelleobama.com. Read from the electronic version; page numbers not included.

chosen to love. An essential part of being yourself according to Obama. We all have families to take care of and passions to support. Obama even brings up a time when her husband missed a flight back to Washington, D.C., to vote on a crime bill because of a sick child. Though professionally it may have been frowned upon, his family was (and is) his core value. And it is these small decisions and sacrifices explored in "Becoming Us," that serve as a nice reminder that as humans, sometimes it's okay to disappoint others, as long as we are following what we truly believe in.

Finally, in "Becoming More," Obama discusses the lack of a guidebook to being the first lady, just as there is no guidebook to navigating life. Pointing this out is the first step to acknowledging that you have to make your own path. During her time as first lady, distributing information on nutrition, the process of food production, and general public health was Obama's priority. Unfortunately, the world around her took more notice to what she was wearing than what she cared to address. To combat this, Obama made a point to present herself well—she even got a 'glam squad'—in hopes that the public would notice the initiatives she was promoting as much as her image.

From a young age, Obama was encouraged to learn and advocate for herself. In fact, this mandate became another platform of hers, along with advocating for female role models, while in the White House. Over time, she came to realize not all children had the advantage of being helped at home. This lack of guidance caused some children to be devalued at school. She states, "Hearing them, I realized that [those with at-home guidance] weren't at all smarter than the rest of us. They were simply emboldened, floating on an ancient tide of superiority, buoyed by the fact that history had never told them anything different." A desire to impress (to emulate) can lead a child to accomplish things they may not have had the drive to do alone. Not only do her initiatives teach children the skills they are seeking out, but also the confidence to succeed in areas and situations they may feel intimidated by, rather than doubtful of their own worth. Obama wanted to make sure children who may have hidden potentials have the chance to speak and be heard through advocacy and mentoring programs.

In *Becoming*, she expresses that, growing up, her family was a group of planners, which made her an avid planner as well. Throughout the book though, she does not shy away from recalling difficult scenarios she was unable to plan around. In her mid 20s, she lost both a good friend and her father close together. Around the same time, she was assigned to be Barack's mentor at a Chicago law firm, Sidley Austin LLP; at first she was less than impressed by him, but over time began to fall in love, changing the course of her career and the life she had originally planned. Though she studied her hardest, at one point, she even failed the Illinois bar on her first try. And, in her mid 30s, she even had to go through the heartbreak of a miscarriage.

Though these events are hard to read about, especially at a time like we are currently experiencing, and as a planner myself, it does offer a sense of comfort. There is a vast amount of ideas currently evolving around us, in our country and culture, that have to be taken in stride. But we can plan only day by day and take the unexpected on the chin. We aren't perfect, we are just ourselves. These stories she presents, and *Becoming* itself, explore the fact that we need to get rid of the failing stigma in order to truly succeed. We can try to plan, but sometimes the universe has its own plan. People function better when honest, when we express our downfalls, rather than when we put up a front and go through trauma alone.

In owning your true self, you need to allow your mind to wander at night, be it thinking about a lost relative or income inequalities. You must own your story. No one else can for you. Approach the world as it should be, rather than complain about the world as it is. That's how change is created. We learn from each other, and in learning we transform. "Becoming isn't about arriving somewhere or achieving a certain aim," Obama writes. "I see it instead as a forward motion, a means of evolving, a way to reach continuously toward a better self. The journey doesn't end." In other words, never stop changing in order to continue being (becoming) true to your genuine self. Never stop reforming.

Be You, Beautiful
Nikita Rimal Sharma

Have you ever wondered what would happen
if the sun ever doubted itself,
on days it didn't shine as bright?
What if the moon felt shattered,
on nights it didn't light up the whole sky?
Would they ever come back,
if they spent their time blaming the clouds,
for getting in the way?

What if the mountains never wanted to take up space,
and the flowers didn't see the point in blooming fully?
What if rivers and oceans decided not to flow,
and the birds thought their singing wasn't worth listening to?

Have you ever also wondered, darling,
what would happen,
if like the sun you rose,
if like the mountains, you stood tall,
if like the river you flowed,
Wholeheartedly, Undoubtedly?

reformation : revision/reformulation

Stereotactic
Katie Mitchell

"Now hold your breath," the radiologist instructs as the machine hums. I dutifully follow her command, clenching my jaw as I pause mid exhale. I listen to her mumble numbers and terms to the technician, talking about my body in words I cannot understand. This is a stereotactic biopsy, I'd learned. Under the guidance of a mammogram machine, they are using a needle to extract a portion of my breast and then placing a tiny titanium pin inside of me to mark the spot.

I am facedown and shirtless in a sterile hospital room with my head craned sharply to the right where I stare at the blank wall. My bare breast is hanging through a hole in the table, dangling over the head of the radiologist seated below. I wonder what it looks like, my small B-cup shape, hanging down like that, a sharply pointed triangle hovering above her. Only men have seen this view before, looking up at me in our most intimate moments, not in a brightly lit and sterile place. I keep my focus on the blank wall, motionless, listening to them call out unknown coordinates and medical terms.

This journey all began two months ago with a simple baseline mammogram. "You are 37?" my midwife asked as she flipped through my chart at my annual appointment. "We usually suggest a baseline image now so that we have something to compare it to later." I scheduled an appointment later that week. I found myself wrapped in a pink robe walking down a long hallway and into a small room where I stripped the robe off and stood still for the cold machine to squeeze and flatten each side. I held my breath until they told me to exhale. Then I got dressed and left.

Days later the clinic called back to explain they needed another image to see through the dense tissue. I obliged, by now an expert at stilling my breath for the machines. Then another call came insisting on a biopsy to check a concerning spot buried far beneath what I could feel with my own hands. I repeated the terms to myself—*young, no family history*—and rolled my eyes at the over-precaution of modern medicine. But even though I tried, I could not forget the clipped way the doctor had said the words **BIOPSY** and **CONCERNING**. When I didn't make the appointment, they called a week later. **BIOPSY** and **CONCERNING**, I hear it again. The week after the second mammogram, my daughter climbed into bed with me at 2:00 a.m. And as I felt the weight of her arm across my waist in the darkness and her sleeping breath on my neck, I decided to reconsider the biopsy.

Sunday afternoon came. I sat at a restaurant table across from the man I was dating. He had a head full of thick salt and pepper hair and serious eyes. We shared guacamole and icy margaritas in the sunshine, and I told him about my biopsy. He tilted his head and furrowed his brow. But he didn't flinch (*this is why I think I love him, because he doesn't flinch*).

Our first date had been five months prior, and even in that first hour, I recognized something in his eyes that felt strangely familiar, a mirror of my own. I described him to my friends by giving him praise for doing all the things that I do—parenting two small kids, packing the lunches, calling the pediatrician, kissing their sleeping cheeks in his quiet house. He seemed like a relic from another time, opening every door for me, rarely sending hurried text messages, calling me instead. On our third date, we stumbled in the darkness of a historic graveyard on a ghost tour and drank midnight coffee, talking about all the ways life broke us. We shared our first kiss that night on a parking deck, and he giggled as much as I did at the quiet heat of it all.

We finished the guacamole and he told me that he knew where I could go for a second opinion, if I wanted one. "False alarms happen all the time," he said. "All the time. But these doctors are the best. They will take care of you, and when you get the bill from the lab, you can ignore it. You won't have to pay. It's the company I work for, so you won't have to worry about it." He'd spent a decade in medical sales working with women's health providers. It was another reason I felt I loved him.

The last time I saw him, we ate fish tacos served on little metal trays lined with parchment paper and shared salted fries from a basket. We strolled hand in hand to the movie theater and sat on a bench with his arm lazily draped over my shoulders, laughing at the drunk girls who asked me to take their picture. We shared midnight coffee again and one tall slice of chocolate cake at our usual spot. The night ended between his sheets. I ran my fingers across his chest as we talked, and studied the lines around his eyes as he smiled. He walked me to my car and hugged me tightly and told me to call him when I got home. I did, feeling his hand on my shoulder from far away, keeping me safe from dark curvy roads and biopsies and all the things I carried.

Nine days of silence followed that night. I knew, I'd experienced this before, the man who disappears. It is the man I know best. On that day nine, he sent a text message (did not call) to casually explain that though I'm lovely, he found someone else.

The next day, Brett Kavanaugh was shouting on the news, and my stomach burned with Christine Blasey Ford's testimony and with his response and with all of it. I decided perhaps I was lucky after all. I had never had anything taken from me by force. I willingly give myself, and it does not leave physical trauma in its path. Instead it is just a tender, aching spot in the empty space a man occupied, pulsing like a phantom.

I had made my appointment with his suggested breast specialist just before he disappeared, so by the time I sat on the chair in their office with the stack of patient intake forms on a clipboard, he was gone. I left the "referred by" line blank. I wrapped myself in the flimsy gown again and listened to a new voice tell me the same terms—**BIOPSY** and **CONCERNING**. So when the day came, I drove to the nearby hospital, took an elevator to the fourth floor, walked down the long hallway, and laid on the table to let my breast dangle above the radiologist and let the needle go in. And stare at a blank wall.

Finally, the tests are done, and the radiologist leaves the room after placing petri dishes in the refrigerator. I watch her place them on the shelf, tiny pieces of me inside. The technician remains behind to hold compression on my breast for a while. "We like to get this bleeding to stop before you leave," she explains. I move my stiff neck as best I can and inhale deeply, but I stay facedown on the table with the hole and her remaining beneath me. She apologizes that it is taking so long to stop the bleeding.

She begins to give me instructions and implies that there is a husband in my house who will need to be sensitive to the bruising and leave my breast alone for a while. I explain to her that it won't be a problem as I sleep alone. She asks how old my kids are and how they handle it and if they see their dad often. I answer yes and say we are okay.

"I know you are tired," she says.

I'm glad to be staring at this empty wall; my eyes overflow. I mumble that yes, sometimes I'm tired. She tells me that she divorced years ago and that last year her mother died of Alzheimer's. "Sometimes life hands you a lot and your body gets tired," she says. She is still holding pressure on my breast, dangling above her like a tiny trapeze. "I'm so sorry about your mom," I tell her while she squeezes my breast tenderly with a bloodstained handful of gauze.

She tells me that I can sit up now, and I do. I'm still elevated on the table just above her so that her head is level with my breast. I watch her eyelashes behind the surgical goggles and listen to the clanging silver bracelets on her arm as she carefully cleans the last bit of blood with a warm cloth. She notices that I am shivering and places the hospital gown over my shoulders like a shawl. When we are done, she guides me to another room with bare walls, and I sit on another table. This time it's the familiar kind with a paper cover and no hole. She leaves for a moment to take the images to the doctor for one last look at the small metal pin and I swallow the hard lump in my throat. She finally returns to give me an ice pack for my bra and a list of written instructions. She hugs me, and I struggle to say thank you without my voice breaking. This sister, this stranger.

When I get home, the kids are in the neighbor's backyard bouncing on the trampoline in the bright fall sunshine. I do what I was told in the days ahead, apply the ice pack, change the bandage, and on day five I remove the surgical tape and rinse off the dried blood in a hot shower. My breast is one big bruise that changes colors everyday like a kaleidoscope—red and purple and pink and brown and green. My daughter stares at it as I step from the shower.

"Does it hurt, Mommy?"

"Not anymore," I tell her, though I still feel the soreness beneath my fingers when I try to touch it.

And on that fifth day, I carry my phone everywhere with the ringer on. I say I am not nervous, but I am waiting and wondering and hardening my stomach for whatever news they will have to tell me. As I sit down with my coworker at our favorite lunch spot, it finally rings. I step outside in the parking lot to hear that word **BENIGN**, and I exhale. I come back to the table with a wide smile, and we share a piece of pie to celebrate. My breast is still dark and sore to the touch.

As I undress that night, I look in the mirror and see the purple stain tinged with green stretching the length of my breast below my tender nipple. I imagine the tiny pin forever inside of me. I think about the table in the sterile room, the kind technician, the bloody petri dish. I think about our midnight coffee, his careful hand on my shoulder, his serious eyes. I remember the way he always moved me to the inside of the sidewalk to stand between my body and the parallel traffic. **BENIGN**. I say the word aloud again to the mirror so I can hear it in my own voice and convince myself it is true.

reformation : transition

On hiking alone as a woman
Anna Nissley

To escape isn't looking over your shoulder.
It's not holding your breath.
It's not wondering
whether the steps behind you
are getting louder.
Healing isn't envisioning
fifty ways to kick and scream.
Healing doesn't live in suggestions to bring a friend.

To heal
is a privilege—
to escape is a dream.

I stand on the furthest rock
jutting chin and belief of belonging
into the air to
make them true.

reformation : unlearning/
self-actualization

The Body and the Boy
Saige Thornley

And he taught me about the slow hours that come in the morning
When the whole world seems to fade away.
When these objects of our bodies in rest tend to stay at rest.
Our love was made for the films he took me to,
For the times after he wrapped his arms around me
And called me his home.

But how can he be at home in a body that I, myself,
	cannot call my own?
I do not want to be at war with this body anymore.
This body does not pleasure to be the temple that I need it to be.
There is a reckoning between us.
How can I know a lover before I learn to love myself?

This boy, this force of lightning trapped in a plasma ball,
Came but did not wait for me to call.
I did not mean to provoke this fight; I did not mean to hurt him.
I did not want to put up with his childnesses any longer.
I wake alone in the hours he told me of.
I am a child, dwarfed by the body of the bed that he and I
	used to fill.
I decide that he was the duck's back and I was the water.
I reach for my phone that was flung across the room
In a fit of tears and hurt.
How do I be whole again?

This body does not yet know healing.
Grant me peace,
Grant me grace,
Grant me the patience to be what I need to be.

I remember how long it has taken me to get here.
Healing is not all soup and warm showers, but it does take time.
I sip the tea that tastes like forgiveness,
Call myself home and forget the rest.

reformation : reclamation

The Timidity of Human Toes
Katie Murray

Millions of years have made us. And in that time, you humans have not changed much. You are kinder to each other but not to yourselves. We beckon you; can you feel it? You love the sound of us. And we love watching you.

We waterfalls are empaths—it must be all the water rushing through us. We have an instinct about which thoughts to hold onto and which to let rush on by, to abandon with a frothy flourish into the dark depths below. The strangled tides inside you need something only water can give; the vortex of your thoughts is so unlike our faultless streams.

Everything comes crashing through us; there can be no tucking of secret thoughts away, to chew over later, while fingering blue-bruised edges. With your hangnails bitter in your mouths, you humans are always checking for pain, letting metallic, bloody thoughts stew. We release all. Even the thoughts you may find ugly.

Now, I'll let you in on a little secret: human feet are of the utmost interest to waterfalls and rock pools. Some feet are skittish, some unsteady, some firm and knowing. You can feel so much sometimes just in a footprint—the way the sole is or is not pressed to the stone's surface; the timidity of human toes can reveal so much. It can be heartbreaking for us, to bear witness, to soak up your soles. Although we do love a drama—especially a tragedy— we are not intentionally cruel; we do not delight in the traumas and twisted tales humans bring to us constantly. The incessant ebb and flow of human discontent: the murky kind, the oily kind, the kind that seeps out of soles sometimes. It can make a waterfall uncomfortable, uneasy even, to watch while humans dwell so deeply and completely.

Let the pain go, we urge. It has already passed.

But not many of you listen. We cannot feel the past like you do; it does not exist for us. We cannot hold old moments in our hearts and minds, to look at from every angle, to scrutinise, to replay. The past for us is simply more pressure. Or a particularly grand rock. We hold no memories, no images, no flashbacks that appear as photographs but could never really be. We live inside the burst of fresh currents—white frothed abandonment.

Here comes a human now! She has a heart and an ear for the water and a look in her flecked blue-green eyes that is not quite sadness and not quite despair. But a pooling mixture of the two.

You can see that despite whatever she has had to endure, her feet are steady and strong; we like that. Pure as bones and wholesome thoughts, we lie here still and cold; the stones glint and whisper to her suntanned feet. She places her sole slowly and deliberately across each of our mossy rocks and the chipped coral polish on her toenails shines iridescent in the late afternoon light. Dappled and luminous green, all shades at once—an enchanting sight. We can see how that sends a hum of contentment right through her heart. A well-done sum. Makes her feel as though she fits in somewhere (in her own life). Before she's fully registered the usual dark well of fear, one brown foot is in front of the other and she's carving out a wobbly but purposeful path to the top of our crest.

Ah, she's one of those humans, our favourite kind, always seeking counsel from water. It doesn't matter if it's the roaring sea, the roiling river, or the millpond lake—water soothes something deep within her. It is palpable. Each step is careful. We feel a lightness in the spring of her toes and glimmer appreciatively. Craggy rocks black and green and all the ferns in between urge her on. The pressure of us all surges against the back of her heels, naked ankles still a storm as impatient water reforms its own path; the impetuous rush over once-ragged rocks. Down. Down. Down. Always down. Where else is there?

Moments crack open and reveal their truth. The top is daunting. It is beautiful. She cocks her head and we know she will listen.

Feel it all, we urge. The rush and the sadness. The loneliness and the doubt. Be it all. The beauty and the love. The brutality and the fear. Mayhem and wonder. Inexplicable loss and unbounded growth. Feel it all. Our power only swells with more water, with more stones and rocks in our path. Like you. Nothing can stop you. Just make sure you feel it all.

And feel the anger. The white-tipped sorrow. And the roiling loss. Feel it all. Joy. Loneliness. The craggy bones of a bitter discontent only you can feel. Particles of hope. Sunshine behind your eyelids. Every shade and whisper of green. Others people's bones when you hold them. Warm limbs. Your small hands. Your throat opening like a starling at dusk, unafraid and complete.

As moments crack open, sit inside them. Be the bone-dragging weariness and the flash of life in your very own eyes. Forgive. Yourself. Forgive the world for breaking you. Forgive yourself for holding on to the feelings you do not need. We are always here. Always. Just not ever the same. We are shifting and streaming, never the same, from one moment to the next.

Nothing forgives like water.

reformation : reliving

The Suitcase
Glenna D. Wolfe

burgundy and battered, strained
at its zipper, is delivered, tardy,
to its worried owner, herself two
days arrived to this new world.
Eyes shining, squeaking with joy
she opens her treasure—out spill
pictures of her children as babies,
a small packet of spices, beads
once worn by her mother, a recipe
in her aunt's hand. She pats
a small stash of clean rags—her
washcloths or handkerchiefs or
her monthly pads. Her son's
green yo-yo rolls by, a plastic
doll peers over a sweater. There
is needle and thread, a Bible—
all relic-seeds to be repotted
in fertile soil.

Alien
Keshni Naicker Washington

AirPods inserted. Mask adjusted. Hands sheathed in blue disposable gloves. After ascending from the underground parking, I launch off the escalator and into the local Safeway as an astronaut would. My solo mission today is to seek out and acquire missing dinner supplies. I pause and scan the environment right away for obstacles and interceptions. With my path calculations complete, I stride with care. I imagine the digital trail that would be displayed in bright blue dots if I had on an astronaut visor. No artificial intelligence illuminates my prescription lenses in the tortoiseshell frames that rest on my nose. From Warby Parker. A few strides ahead, a local halts with no prior warning. He hovers in indecision and blocks off the entrance to the cereal aisle, my next destination. Evasive maneuvers are deployed with success as I veer wide and pass.

The fine hairs on my forearms rise as I enter the frozen straits of the refrigerated and fresh produce islands. I locate and collect my samples. Cheese and margarine are plucked from a wall of illuminated choices. Then I find the limes, bananas, and cucumbers. An island covered in mounds of orange spheres draws me in, as if I am caught in a tractor beam. *Am I seeing correctly*? I reach out blue fingers and unfold the tag. Cara Cara oranges. All the way from South Africa. All the way from home.

The restrictions of the Green Card application process have held me within these borders, unable to return home for a visit, for the past three years and counting. Memories squeeze my heart as I haul the sack into my basket. My latex encased finger traces the pattern of the red netting. Beneath my face covering, a smile emerges. A long-forgotten memory transports me back to childhood. A familiar sharp chemical scent and scraping on my skin accompanies it. I remember the green bar of no-nonsense soap, and the even less nonsense-way it was applied to my younger form, during bucket baths with a sack exactly like this one. Being the oldest of three, I was often scolded into setting a good example for my little brother and sister. I held in my yelps and funny faces and bossed them around despite us only being a few years apart in age. In the humble homes of the apartheid segregated township of Chatsworth in KwaZulu Natal where I was raised, people did much with little.

Having served its first duty of holding onions or oranges, the sack was reformed into a bath-time implement. I glance at my basket and chuckle. Never assume that the margarine tubs you see in those aunties' fridges contain what's emblazoned on the outside of the container. The plastic tubs, whether margarine or ice-cream in their first life, gain a second life in Chatsworth holding anything from ground-down herb pastes to oiled and spiced vegetable pickles.

As I head toward the registers with my Safeway basket full of loot (including the tasty oranges), the reignited longing inside me grows heavier with each step. In some ways, growing up in Africa might as well be like growing up on another planet. My American reformation began as a natural ebb of old habits slowly substituted with foreign influences. **TOM-MAR-TOE** changed to **TOM-MAY-TO**. Teatime changed to coffee-time. Vitamin D supplements now replace the year-round sunshine that used to bathe my brown skin. My usual array of spices like turmeric, garam, cumin, and cloves omitted from meals to make them more palatable to American tongues. After almost a decade in Washington, D.C., I have accepted that my birthday marks the beginning of fall here, whereas it used to herald the start of southern hemisphere spring in my previous home.

Many things make me an alien here. My different relationship with the red sack of oranges is the least of them. But an astronaut must brave the vast loneliness to explore strange new lands. Her tongue must be ready to mold to new languages. Her body must be ready to adapt to different gravity. And in the midst of all this difference, her mind must stay open to discoveries she can't yet imagine but have the potential to enrich all that has come before.

I insert a plastic rectangle into a device. Numbers scroll across a screen. Something clicks. A strip of paper is ejected. The exchange of money for samples is complete. As I stand again on the mechanically descending staircase that now takes me back underground, the flow of substitution reverses. The oranges and the unusual spices call to me once more. I mentally ransack the inventory of my kitchen cupboard. Yes, my husband will be introduced to a South African chakalaka variation on pizza tonight.

reformation : reclamation

Fearless
Chris Biles

You look out the window
naked
morning light flooding through
the chasm
created
by your pulling back
of the curtains

Your body
is fearless

I wonder
if you make it a habit
of pulling back curtains
of letting in the light

We are deep
here
together
we may get lost
but
stretching
into every corner
the light reaches
and you are there
showing me
that the sum of all
my flaws

is beauty
is sunrise on skin
is skin
freed
from clothing's confines
is your fearless body
illuminated
by the light of day
is mine

(re)formation : renewal

Book Review
World of Wonders: In Praise of Fireflies, Whale Sharks, and Other Astonishments
by Aimee Nezhukumatathil
Reviewed by Siobhan McKenna

Catalpa trees or *catalpa speciosa* can grow to be almost 60 ft tall, have "foot-long leaves," and "can give two brown girls in western Kansas a green umbrella from the sun" (1). So begins Aimee Nezhukumatathil in the first essay of *World of Wonders: In Praise of Fireflies, Whale Sharks, and Other Astonishments.*[1] This book of 28 lyrical essays weaves together fascinating tidbits about species in our natural world with Nezhukumatathil's own journey of finding self-acceptance and the meaning of living in a country where being 'other' must be navigated on a daily basis. Through the essays, characteristics found within nature reflect Nezhukumatathil's own qualities as she moves through everyday life.

In her included essays—most titled after a natural wonder and its scientific name—Nezhukumatathil acts as the narrator of a National Geographic documentary. As our guide, she begins in the landscape of her youth where she realized that growing up with a Filipina mother and Indian father set her apart from other children and would color nearly every aspect of her life in the years to come. From there, she whisks the reader from the sweet fields of love as she knew her husband was the one when he "didn't blanch" at her adoration for the corpse flower (whose scent is reminiscent of "a used diaper pail left out in the late August sun" (70)) to the depths of motherhood where in swimming with a whale shark, she realized that she was "unprepared to submit [herself] so completely to nature" (89) with the implications of the worst occurring: a motherless son.

---

1 Published by Milkweed Editions (2020), 184 pages; hardcover (978-1-5713136-5-2) or e-book (978-1-5713195-9-3). For more information, visit milkweed.org/book/world-of-wonders.

Nezhukumatathil, an author of four other collections of poetry, spellbinds the reader with her sensory imagery. She compares the petals of a touch-me-not to something that "look[s] as if someone crossed a My Little Pony doll with a tiny firework" (25) and envelops the reader in the smell of a monsoon: like the "wind off the wings of an ecstatic teeny bat" mixed with "banana leaves drooping low," and "clouds whirring so fast across the sky" (58–59). In fact, every essay is saturated in lush prose that transports the reader alongside Nezhukumatathil as she is slowly sipping a dragon fruit cocktail in "Mississippi when the air outside is like a napping dragon's exhalations" (115).

But the beauty found in her lyricism does not detract from the gravitas of the messages that underlies her essays. As a daughter of immigrant parents, Nezhukumatathil calls us to be better to one another when faced with diversity and to not succumb to tropes where racism can be chalked up as a sign of older times or the ignorance of children.

In her essay "*Monodon monoceros*," she speaks of channeling the narwhal's preference for swimming through "chunky ice rather than open seas" (35–36) when a boy on her school bus "flipped his eyelids inside out" (38) after she explained to him that her mom was in fact Filipino and not Chinese. And in "*Ambystoma mexicanum*," she presents that remembering the smile of an axolotl (thin and tough) "can help you smile as an adult even if someone on your tenure committee puts his palms together as if in prayer every time he sees you off-campus, and does a quick, short bow, and calls out, *Namaste!*" (45) despite telling him repeatedly that she's Methodist. Nezhukumatathil demands that we alter what we teach our children about those different from ourselves and how we internalize these differences as adults. By illustrating these cringeworthy and far too common microaggressions, she cries for us to be curious, not assumptive about the questions to which we do not know the answers.

Yet, instead of seeking pity, Nezhukumatathil burns with a

firm resolve to find home wherever her feet seep into the soil by calling on the natural world around her. Similar to a red-spotted newt, which takes time "wandering the forest floor before it decides which pond to call home" (139), Nezhukumatathil moved from places such as Arizona, Iowa, and Western New York, before settling in Mississippi with her husband. And although her move from Western New York was precipitated after she became weary "of acquaintances at the post office asking about 'my people,'" she wonders what would have happened if she saw a red-spotted newt in the midst of a bleak New York winter "skittering under the surface of the ice" (142) as they often do. Like the perseverant newt, Nezhukumatathil thinks she might have stayed, calling to mind that "all this time, my immigrant parents had been preparing me to find solace in multiple terrains and hoping to create a feeling of home wherever I needed to be in this country" (143).

Nezhukumatathil's disposition toward finding goodness in the face of adversity and using the natural world as a guiding light is what ultimately defines her work and seems especially timely in light of our country's current social and ecological climate. To me, Nezhukumatathil's essays serve as a call to action as unmatched wildfires continue to ravage the west coast and racial discrimination is brought to the front of a long-overdue national conversation. Her skillful synthesis of these intense topics into short digestible anecdotes—while still channeling hope—is the precise writing we need right now for us to feel stirred to work toward the daunting tasks of preserving our earth and dismantling racial injustice in our country.

As the compilation winds down, Nezhukumatathil introduces the reader to a *Casuarius casuarius* or southern cassowary. These flightless birds are native to New Guinea and Australia and are relied upon to preserve biodiversity as a keystone species. Most interestingly, Nezhukumatathil teaches us, in her colorful, rhythmic prose, cassowaries have a call that can't be heard by humans, but only felt—a "rumble" (148) deep in our bones. She ponders on this feeling: "suppose that boom shaking in our body can be a physical reminder that we are all connected" (149). This musing echoes again and again as the reader encounters each creature and sees a reflection of themselves staring back. Because, Nezhukumatathil warns, in order to reform how we commune with human beings—nature—we must remember that all that is precious in our world will be lost if we do not slow down and feel the vibrations of the earth; feel the beat of each other's hearts.

reformation : restoration

Sanctuary
Paulina Freedman

A small girl cowers alone.
No one ever sees her cry
in the cave that's all her own.

An owl hoots a calming tone;
the one that she is guarded by
while she hides out all alone.

Surrounded by sand and stone
and winged birds, a girl can fly
around the shelter all her own.

Out of truth she carves her throne,
for no one ever tells a lie
to the quiet girl who endures alone.

With silk and strength she weaves her gown,
a glint of magic in her eye,
in the sanctuary all her own.

Moonlight melts into her bones.
Even the stars don't dare defy
the steadfast girl who shines alone,
in a kingdom all her own.

formation : genesis

Book Review
The Indomitable Florence Finch: The Untold Story of a War Widow Turned Resistance Fighter and Savior of American POWs
by Robert J. Mrazek
Reviewed by Charity R. Bartley Howard

Florence Ebersole Finch (1915–2016) lived a fascinating and important life. *The Indomitable Florence Finch: The Untold Story of a War Widow Turned Resistance Fighter and Savior of American POWs* by Robert J. Mrazek[1] is the true telling of the life of a hero many may not have heard of before. Florence Finch saved many American lives (prisoners of war or POWs) in the Philippines during World War II. The Americans were in the country starting in early 1942 to mid to late 1945. Their goal was to help the Filipino campaign against Japanese forces, to stop Japan from occupying the area. Now, with this engaging book, her story is finally being told. Florence was humble during and after the war, and her efforts were not for the sake of glory, but rather what she felt was necessary and right.

This is an exceptionally written biography about an exceptional person. Mrazek worked from personal journals, taped interviews, and other original sources. The information was compiled from the past experiences of an elderly woman who finally explained everything to her family only a few years before she died in 2016 at age 101. Born to a Filipina woman and an American serviceman in 1915, Florence was raised in the Philippines and married an American sailor, Charles Smith. She had worked for the U.S. Army in Manila in 1941 prior to the Japanese invasion of the Philippines; it is there she met her husband. Unfortunately, he would be killed

---

1 Published by Hachette Books (2020), 368 pages; hardcover (978-0-3164222-7-7) or e-book (978-0-3164222-4-6). For more information, visit robertjmrazek.com/florencefinch.html.

in action in the Philippines in 1942, and she soon found herself a widow within the Japanese-occupied Philippines.

At the start of occupation, Florence had taken a job at the Philippine Liquid Fuel Distribution Union (controlled by the Japanese). For two years, this led her to slyly helping the Philippine resistance against the Japanese in many ways: diverting fuel shipments, falsifying documents, and obtaining supplies for POWs. In 1944, her actions were discovered; Florence was arrested, tortured, tried, and sentenced to three years of imprisonment. She remained in captivity until American troops liberated the Philippines in 1945.

Mrazek's book does her justice. While at the beginning it might take readers some time to get into the story and stay with it, learning the background is important to knowing the full scope of Florence's remarkable life and achievements. Readers are given vivid details as well as facts from her time during and before the war, creating a delightful read for those who appreciate history and learning about an unsung hero. Ultimately, this is a story of a remarkable woman all readers can admire. Florence was awarded the American Medal of Freedom in 1947 and was the first woman given the Asiatic-Pacific Campaign Ribbon. In 1995, the Coast Guard (who she worked for after the war) named a building on Sand Island in Hawai'i in her honor. Without her efforts, many family members would have lost their loved ones, making her sacrifices important.

Not all war heroes are on the frontlines or are known to us today. In *The Indomitable Florence Finch*, readers hear the account of one of these unknown heroes. Mrazek's account is real without being overly violent, but accurately explains what happened. Readers journey in triumph and sadness, both through her war efforts and through her personal tragedies. It helps us understand what happened before us and the sacrifices people made that allow us to live the way we do today. Knowing about her and how she was selfless sets a good example of how we should care about as well as help others. Pertinent information given our current worldwide situation.

Florence lived an interesting and heart-breaking life, full of incredible bravery. Mrazek does a superb job of interweaving the historical narrative of World War II with Florence Finch's personal life, into an engaging as well as emotional book. *The Indomitable Florence Finch* also relates an element of World War II many may not have much knowledge of, but will have a better understanding of, following this dramatic telling of Florence's experiences. There are many other stories yet to tell of brave women, and men, throughout history. If you are interested in learning more about an unsung woman hero in history, this is a well-told story of Florence Finch's brave efforts and strengths. It is an emotional story that was needed and done in a wonderful way. This is a must read for everyone.

reformation : reorientation/ regrouping

my reformation
RC deWinter

i miss the
me i used to be
the smiling
jester with
the knife playing to the crowd
silent until the

exact right
moment to hurl it
well aimed to
deliver
the coup de grâce to a fool
bloodletting was my

sport and i
never felt remorse
looking back
i wonder
that people put up with me
and my arsenal

of verbal
weapons but it was
not today
when our
horizons have been enlarged
and empathy is

the new badge
of honor and i get
it we all
bleed red but
still there are things done and said
that deserve the slings

and arrows
so having enlarged
myself to
embrace the
empathy necessary
on the global stage

i now bite
my tongue until it
bleeds saving
the best of
my worst for the real villains
herding the rest of

us onto
the margins where we
teeter and
sometimes fall
into the boundless pit of the
forgettable the new

serfs useful
until we can no
longer pull
the plow then
abandoned to survive best we
can and many don't

i still cringe
at the ignorance
of others
their dizzy
hopefulness their fuzzy math
the shopworn belief

that good will
be rewarded and
evil will
be punished
but i don't blood them as i
i would have when i

was young and
ignorant in the
arrogance
of beauty
if i can't reach them with facts
i leave them to their

delusions
we all go to hell
in our own
way and though
mine has become much duller
i'm better for it

Somebody Else's Movie
Aressa V. Williams

If you are assigned the role victim in somebody else's movie,
Don't show up for rehearsal.

A certain group of people want us to feel
Angry, bullied, confused, inferior, unhappy.
Sufferers drawn in their drama.

The coworker parks in your reserved spot.
On purpose.
Become a comedian; flip the script.
Apologize as if you are parking in his space.

The English teacher copies your classroom bulletin boards.
Ask her about it, you are a liar, troublemaker.
Be a mime, say nothing.
Change your bulletin board
(For every stolen idea, you have 50 more).

Family user-takers never contribute to dinners, celebrations,
Show up with greedy friends, take home doggie bags.
Create new lines; change the scene.
When vultures call to find out where and when,
"Everybody pays for his own meal at Jaspers."

The next-door neighbor complains about your cedar shrub.
"It spreads to my side and makes my lawn look untidy."
Agree, apologize.
Become a set designer.
Replace the shrub with a decorative container of flowers.

Feel attacked, disrespected, sad, taken-advantage-of
In somebody else's movie?
Don't go on stage.

reformation : change/
improve/restructure

A Walk in the Park
Amy L. Bernstein

I drag my old white body wherever.
The park—prettified specifically for me:
neat asphalt trails,
thick stands of white oak and holly,
shafting sunlight, picnic tables, pavilions,
and no Black bodies here today, between
Locust Cove and the Chesapeake Bay.

Long before me,
the parkland "belonged" to Mr. T,
his beloved Rocky Beach an enclave of
private pleasure palaces and boat slips.
Mr. T of the Baltimore Leaf Tobacco Association,
of barns, granaries, water, and electric plants,
of four private country clubs
where surely there were Black bodies aplenty.

Before that,
Mr. T's daddy stood with General Loring in the
    Romney Expedition
under Stonewall Jackson,
oh but keep in mind Mr. T received a gold medal
for rescuing a partially blind colored woman
who fell off a steamboat on the Rappahannock in 1900—
highlight of his obituary

Before that,
Charles Carroll, signer-on to
We hold these truths to be self-evident,
    that all men are created equal,

"bought" the land, of which the park is
but a speck

Before that,
enslaved Black bodies moved logs from Bodkin Creek to
Locust Cove to the Bay,
for commerce and convenience

Before that,
Patuxent and Piscataway, indigenous villagers,
sharpened their spears on the fishing grounds of the cove's
    V-shaped canal.

I drag my old white body wherever,
wending, wending the park's genteel walkways
sculpted to pleasure me
on a warm summer day,
and there are no Black bodies here today to remind me
of where I really am
and who is really here
and to whom I am owing.

reformation : reconsideration

future
Kathryn Sadakierski

we will not be the same
now
after
these days of uncertainty,
when we will hear echoes,
recalling our past selves,
how we lived blissfully,
unknowing,
until
then,
the moment it became clearer
that nothing could remain
forever.

you step into the shadow
of footprints you left behind
only to find
your new prints don't fit,
old and new
collide.
there is this sharp knowledge
of the bittersweet,
like a favorite childhood dish
that now tastes only of grit,
not how
you once
remembered it.

going forward,
how could we forget
who we once were?
what used to be?
echoes from before
are so difficult
to ignore.
while we grow
more aware, more cautious,
knowing we are living history,
in ghost towns no longer unknown
to us,
we are more understanding
of why we must seize the day,
the time we have
to change.

we don't lose
our memories
that return and remind,
evoke and eviscerate,
not leaving our emotions unscathed,
no stone unturned.
history reverberates,
begging us not to repeat it,
but to be better this time,
to save more lives,
hearing the voice of reason
each time we decide.

so we listen,
looking within
at all of these
remembrances.

reformation : rebuilding

Phoenix
Colleen Anderson

I am burning all my poems
The embers will glow for years
just as I, once fueled with words

When the pit is cold
I will take the ashes, rub them in
reanoint my flesh
wait for the phrases to rise again

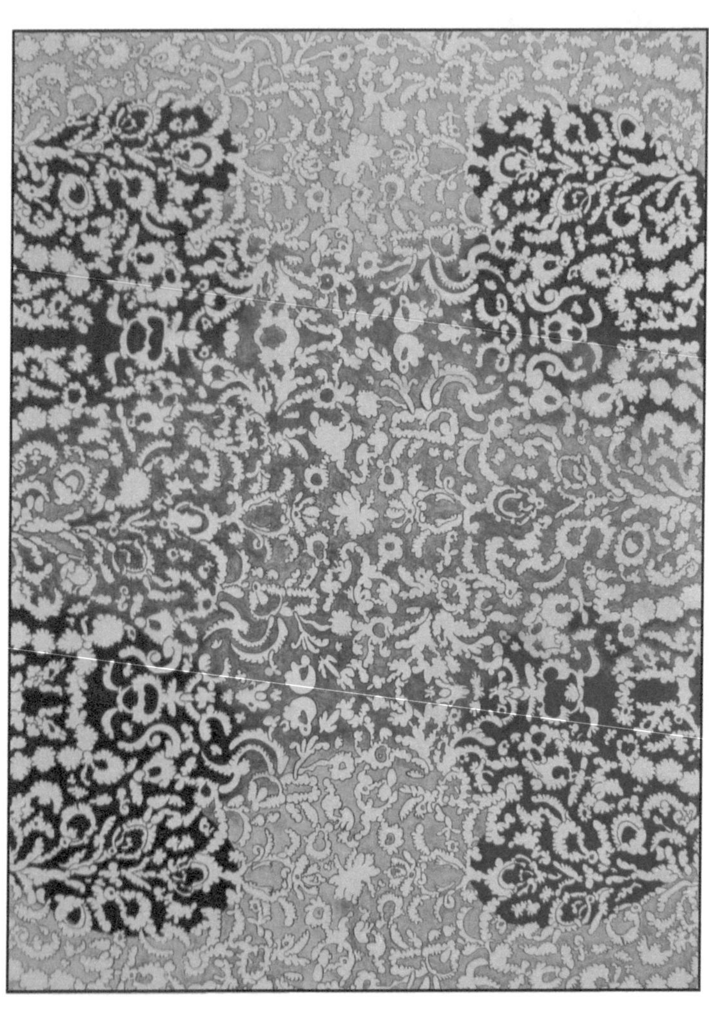

On the Cover: Lace Drawing
Jeanne Quinn

2018 (detail on cover)
graphite and ink on paper, 26 x 19"

Lace Drawing was based on a photograph of a piece of lace that my mother sent to me, some years ago. This piece was the genesis for a long series of works about lace, including large installations made with ceramics and others made with cut vinyl and wire.

I am fascinated by lace. It is firmly nested in the realm of the feminine. Lace is made from one long, continuous line, which creates infinite variations of form. On clothing, it can symbolize many different things, but is closely associated with lingerie (sex) and mourning veils (death). Lace is incredibly strong and requires astonishing commitment—seemingly endless labor—to make by hand.

Lace as a subject reveals something about the theme of (re)formation, in referencing creation and destruction (sex and death), and how it takes a line and turns it into form. Making a drawing of lace takes it from the realm of matter into that of an image, dematerializing this labored textile.

(re)formation : creation—destruction

Contributors

Colleen Anderson has a BFA in writing and her poems have been published in such venues as *Mirror Dance*, *Polu Texni*, *The Future Fire*, and *HWA Poetry Showcase*. She is a Canada Council and BC Arts Council grant recipient for writing and has performed her work before audiences in the U.S., U.K., and Canada. Nominated for the Rhysling, Dwarf Stars, and Aurora Awards for poetry, Colleen's poetry collection, *I Dreamed a World*, will be published in late 2020/early 2021. Colleen has served on numerous HWA and British Fantasy Society juries, and was the 2020 Elgin Awards chair for poetry collections. Find out more about her at colleenanderson.wordpress.com.

Amy L. Bernstein writes about the intersection of politics and culture for the stage and the page. Her novel, *Ell*, will be published in 2021, followed by *The Potrero Complex* in 2022. Selected short plays are published by Routledge and Leicester Bay Theatricals; short fiction by Flying Ketchup Press and Fleas on the Dog; and poetry by Passaic/Voluspa. She is a 2020 finalist for the Petrichor Prize from Regal House Publishing, a 2014 recipient of a Ruby Artist Award from the Greater Baltimore Cultural Alliance, and an award-winning former journalist and executive speechwriter. "A Walk in the Park" is from Amy's unpublished chapbook *White Girl on a Pogo Stick*, which explores reckoning with systemic racism from a white perspective.

Chris Biles currently lives and works in Washington, D.C. She enjoys playing with the light and the dark, and losing herself in music, anything outside, and of course some words here and there. Chris has been published in *Blueline Magazine*, *Signatures Lit and Arts Magazine*, *Words and Whispers*, *The Clementine Zine*, *Fleas on the Dog*, *FEED Lit Mag*, and on SLiPnet. Find her at chrisbiles03.com or on Instagram @marks.in.the.sand.

Ute Carson, a German-born writer from youth, has published two novels, a novella, a volume of stories, four collections of poetry, and numerous essays, here and abroad. Her poetry was twice nominated for the Pushcart Prize. She resides in Austin, Texas with her husband. They have three daughters, six grandchildren, a horse, and a clowder of cats. Please visit her at utecarson.com.

Chiazo V. is a creative writer and author from Nigeria. She wrote and self-published her first book, *The Five Lives of Me*, in 2019. She has been a member of FaithWriters.com, writing on the platform for a number of months. A lot of her work is inspired by real-life situations and personal experiences. Some of her work has been published on Treadbikely, a site for biking enthusiasts. She lives in Abakaliki in Ebonyi State (South Eastern Nigeria) with her husband and three children. She enjoys a good read, a nice walk, and a hearty conversation.

Meg Crane is a Georgia-born author based in New York City. She loves writing across all genres and mediums, from introspective poetry to off-the-wall novels. When she isn't busy writing, Meg can usually be found binge reading in Central Park, thrift shopping for clothes she doesn't need, or watching horror movies with a good cup of tea.

RC deWinter's poetry is widely anthologized, notably in *Uno: A Poetry Anthology* (April 2002), *New York City Haiku* (February 2017), *Cowboys & Cocktails* (April 2019), *Nature In The Now* (August 2019), *Coffin Bell Two* (March 2020), and *A Headrest for Your Soul* (June 2020); in print in *2River, Adelaide, Door Is A Jar, Event, Genre Urban Arts, Gravitas, Kansas City Voices, Meat For Tea: The Valley Review, the minnesota review, Night Picnic Journal, Prairie Schooner, Reality Break Press*, and *Southword*, among others; and appears in numerous online literary journals.

Bailey Drumm is a fiction writer whose written work has been featured in *Grub Street* and *Welter*, and digital art displayed as the cover art for the 2017 edition of *Welter*. She is an MFA graduate from the Creative Writing and Publishing Arts program at the University of Baltimore. Her collection of short stories, *The Art of Settling*, was published in the spring of 2019 and can be found at bailey-drumm.square.site.

LynneAnne Forest is 79 years old and has written poetry throughout her life. She decided to take her writing more seriously and study formally about crafting poetry. She has studied with writers Ellen Bass, Nicole Zimmerman, and Steve Trenam. She is very pleased that her poem is being published in a literary journal specifically dedicated to allow women writers to be heard and valued.

Priscilla Frake is the author of *Correspondence*, a book of epistolary poems. She has work in *Verse Daily*, *Nimrod*, *The Midwest Quarterly*, *Medical Literary Messenger*, *Carbon Culture Review*, *Spoon River Poetry Review*, and *The New Welsh Review*, among others. Anthology publications include *Weaving the Terrain: 100 Word Southwestern Poems*, *Enchantment of the Ordinary*, and *Women. Period.* Her honors include the Lorene Pouncey Award at the Houston Poetry Festival and a Pushcart Prize nomination. She lives in Asheville, North Carolina, where she is a studio jeweler.

Paulina Freedman is a writer, avid reader, amateur chef, and occasional artist living in the suburbs of Chicago, Illinois. She has an MA in Writing and Publishing from DePaul University, and has studied poetry and fiction writing at the University of Iowa Writers' Workshop. She first fell in love with poetry in her sixth grade humanities class and has been writing it ever since.

Charity R. Bartley Howard lives in central Indiana with her sons and husband. She enjoys time with them outside, camping and hiking. Her degrees are in English and journalism. There is always a book open in her house as she enjoys reading, and family reading time is important as well. Spare time also means editing as well as writing articles, stories, and poems.

Sarah Iler has a poem published in the online literary magazine *The Stirling Spoon* (Issue Two) as well as visual art published in two issues of *Ponder Review*. Most recently, Sarah had a poem published in *William and Mary Review* (Vol. 58) and was featured on Paragraph Planet.

Siobhan McKenna resides in Baltimore, Maryland where, when not writing, she works as a cardiac surgery ICU nurse at Johns Hopkins Hospital. With degrees in writing, biology, and nursing, she enjoys translating her experiences within the hospital into creative nonfiction and poetry.

Katie Mitchell is an English teacher and writer living in northern Georgia. Her work has been published by *Mamalode*, *Huffington Post*, *Injection Journal*, and *Appalachian Review*, among others. As a seventh-generation southerner, she is currently writing a memoir exploring how the changes in her own life have mirrored the evolution of the region itself. She is represented by Folio Literary Management.

Katie Murray is a mother of four, a teacher, a PhD researcher, story teller, dog lover, runner, and a breast cancer survivor. Katie knows how words can create a salve and plant trees on your mindscape—she knows how they heal and how they can help you reform. She believes in the power of stories and the healing scope of nature. Katie loves being in nature: all beaches, forests, woods, clambering around in rivers, and—especially—listening to waterfalls.

Anna Nissley graduated from Kutztown University in the middle of a pandemic and is currently teaching eighth grade English under the same circumstances. Both experiences have been strange but undeniably educational. In her free time, she plans for her anticipated 2021 thru-hike on the Appalachian Trail, cooks without recipes, and tries to find ways to recharge.

Jeanne Quinn is an artist whose practice encompasses installation, ceramics, lighting, drawing, digital fabrication, knitting, cooking, and mothering. She studied art history and baroque music performance at Oberlin College and earned her MFA from the University of Washington. She has exhibited widely, including at the Denver Art Museum, the Milwaukee Art Museum, the Kemper Museum for Contemporary Art, Gyeonggi International Ceramics Biennale, and Art Basel/Design Miami. Jeanne has been awarded residencies at the MacDowell Colony, the European Ceramic Work Centre, and many others. She is a professor in the Department of Art and Art History at the University of Colorado.

Nikita Rimal Sharma was born and raised in Kathmandu, Nepal and moved to the U.S. about seven years ago. She is currently living in Baltimore, Maryland. Nikita works at a mental health nonprofit called B'More Clubhouse. She loves to run slowly and think deeply whenever she can. Writing helps her make sense of herself and her life and she loves it for that. Find her on Instagram @nikita.playwithwords.

Deja Ryland is an emerging writer who has recently graduated with her BS in English from Towson University. With a boundless curiosity she writes to ask questions, reflect on experiences, and start conversations. She loves adventure which sparks her love for reading, writing, traveling, and eating. She currently resides in Baltimore, Maryland.

Kathryn Sadakierski is a 21-year-old writer whose work has appeared in various magazines and literary journals, including *ActiveMuse, Critical Read, DoveTales, Halfway Down the Stairs, Literature Today,* NewPages Blog, *Northern New England Review, Origami Poems Project, Snapdragon: A Journal of Art and Healing,* Spillwords, *The Decadent Review, The Voices Project, Visual Verse, Wax Poetry, Art Magazine,* and elsewhere. Her work is forthcoming in *Auroras & Blossoms, Inkwell Literary Magazine (BLC),* and *seashores: an international journal to share the spirit of haiku.* She graduated summa cum laude with a BA from Bay Path University and is currently pursuing her MS.

Saige Thornley is a queer writer currently living in Taiwan. Sometimes they moonlight as an English teacher but would probably like to be writing instead. They have a pet turtle, a caffeine addiction, and a TBR pile that grows every day.

Keshni Naicker Washington's stories are influenced by the two hemispheres she calls home. Born in Chatsworth, an apartheid segregated township in South Africa, she now also considers Washington, D.C., where she lives with her husband, home. And after eight years here, she has finally gotten used to Orion being the right way up in the night's sky. She is a VONA (Voices of Our Nations Arts Foundation) Workshop Alumnus, organized and cohosted the 2020 Inclusive Literature Conference at The Writer's Center DC, hosts The Signal Fire Series podcast, and runs the @TheImmigrantsOfTheDMV Instagram initiative for KAMA DC. Follow her on Instagram @knwauthor or at keshniwashington.com.

Aressa V. Williams, a retired Assistant Professor of English and a Washington, D.C., public school retiree, is a teacher consultant and poet. Career highlights include an Excellence in Leadership Award for "Classroom Management" workshops at AACC, Who's Who Among America's Teachers, Citation for "Literary Achievement and Dedication to Students" from the D.C. Board of Education, and "Outstanding Achievement in Poetry" from Poetry Nation. Aressa's self-published books are *Soft Shadows*, *The Penny Finder,* and *Pancakes & Chocolate Milk.* She says poems are word snapshots. The poetess is the proud mother of Aaron Coley and the grateful grandmother of Aressa Coley.

Glenna D. Wolfe has lived in the Chapel Hill, North Carolina area for many years although she originated in a halcyon time and place in the Missouri Ozarks. Glenna has poems and essays collected into various anthologies and periodicals. In 2008, her chapbook, *Broad Reach*, was published. She has performed with a cast of writers reading their winning essays in the "Listen to Your Mother" shows at William Peace University in Raleigh, North Carolina, and gives, with other poets, poetry readings in the Triangle Area. In 2019, she completed her book of memoirs for her family.

A Final Note
Gwen Van Velsor

As we celebrate the reformation of Yellow Arrow Publishing amongst the turmoil of this year, I find it important to acknowledge the dark side of being reborn. For many heartfelt reasons, the team decided that the difficult work of dismantling and reimagining our organization was paramount.

Just as we waited in the darkness of our mothers' wombs, so now we wait, shrouded in the unknown, on the precipice of new beginnings.

> "I love the dark hours of my being in which my senses drop into the deep."[1]

For many reasons, both worldly and personal, I currently find myself in a "dark night of the soul" (from John of the Cross). Failure, criticism, disappointment, and loss are all descriptors of this season. I also know, however, that after the dark night, sometimes long and tortuous, filled with monsters even, comes the dawn. Always comes the dawn.

Sometimes our best work is created in the night, in the darkness of our dreams, in the shadows of our fears. And sometimes room is made for other descriptors: grace, acceptance, gratitude, humility. With the first light of day, the pointed teeth melt back into the closet, the spinning of our minds slows, and if breath fills our chests, we are granted a new day.

> "In nurturing creativity we must learn to rest in periods of unknowing."[2]

The light of day has brought reformation to Yellow Arrow. With the closing of Yellow Arrow House, our focus has turned exlusively

---

1 Originally from the *Book for the Hours of Praying* by Rainer Maria Rilke, translated from the German by Robert Bly in *The Selected Poems of Rainer Maria Rilke.*
2 From *The Artist's Rule: Nurturing Your Creative Soul with Monastic Wisdom* by Christine Vaulters Paintner.

to our publications department and our gaze has rested on supporting and inspiring writers identifying as women through access to publication and the literary arts. And while we will not be offering annual journal subscriptions at this time nor printing or binding in house, our developing plans will provide more focus to our authors in order to properly showcase who they are and what they want to say. We will continue to strive to create an inclusive and collaborative experience that allows all women to feel safe to create, take risks, learn, and further their writing and publishing goals.

We are grateful to you all for continuing with us along this journey. May this dark night bring you to your deep places and to the ever-present dawn.